C0-AUZ-729

LETTER-HEADS

to make your point!

LETTER-HEADS

to make your point!

Written and Designed by
Gene Light

Harmony Books/New York

For M.L. and H.K.

Copyright © 1983 Gene Light

All rights reserved. No part of this book may be reproduced or
transmitted in any form or by any means, electronic or
mechanical, including photocopying, recording, or by any
information storage and retrieval system, without permission
in writing from the publisher.

Published by Harmony Books, a division of Crown Publishers,
Inc., One Park Avenue, New York, New York 10016 and
simultaneously in Canada by General Publishing Company
Limited

HARMONY and colophon are trademarks of Crown Publishers,
Inc.

Manufactured in the United States of America

ISBN: 0-517-55079-2
10 9 8 7 6 5 4 3 2 1
First Edition

CONTENTS

Pull out the appropiate
letter. Write or type your
address (or leave it out)
under the letterhead. Add
your brilliant prose and
mail away.

We don't guarantee results,
but you <u>will</u> get attention.

Do you want to send a bar-
rage of letters with the
same letterhead? Go ahead
...you've got our permis-
sion. Just stick the original
in a copying machine. Of
course, we'd much prefer
you to buy more copies of
this book.

Americans Against Answering Machines, inc.

Dear Disembodied Voice,

GET RID OF YOUR DAMN ANSWERING MACHINE!

SIGNED

DISCRIMINATING TV VIEWERS
ASSOCIATION OF AMERICA, INC.

HOW DARE YOU

☐ SHOW ☐ PRESENT ☐ AIR ☐ BROADCAST ☐ PUT ON ☐ ACT IN

SUCH TRASH.

Dear _____ ,

The
Appreciation Society
of America

Absolutely Terrific!

Dear Great One:

The MISDIRECTED BILLING Association

I don't owe you this!!

Dear Ignorant Person:

_____

SIGNED

THE SOCIETY
of DISCRIMINATING READERS

Dear Hack:

WELL DONE!

*Dear*_____,

AS A _____ YOU

☐ STINK   ☐ ARE THE GREATEST

☐ COULD USE LESSONS   ☐ ARE NOT BAD   ☐ NEED WORK

☐ COULD WIN MEDALS   ☐ _____

WHERE'S MY

YOU PROMISED TO DELIVER
BY _____

_____

The "Extremely-Lucky-Me" Organization of America

Dear_____,

YOU ARE THE GREATEST!

Dear _____,

AS A WIFE YOU

- ☐ Are the best
- ☐ Could use lessons
- ☐ Could win medals
- ☐ Make me wish I were single again
- ☐ Make me think of divorce
- ☐ _____

DEAR _____

...as a HUSBAND YOU...

- ☐ are the best
- ☐ could use lessons
- ☐ could win medals
- ☐ make me wish I were single again
- ☐ make me think of divorce
- ☐ _____

Dear Heartless Person,

Dear Heartless Person:

EX·BOYFRIENDS ASSOCIATION

DEAR HEARTLESS ONE:

THE ASSOCIATION OF DISCRIMINATING FILMGOERS, INC.

You have the nerve to call yourself a
DIRECTOR!!!

Dear No-Talent,

THE SOCIETY OF STAGE & SCREEN CRITICS LTD.

You Have the Gall to Call Yourself an
ACTOR!!!

Dear No-Talent,

The Furious Wives Association of America

You have the temerity to call yourself a
HUSBAND!!!

Dear Bastard,

Irate Husbands Society of America

You have the audacity to call yourself a WIFE!!!

Dear Bitch…

THE DISCRIMINATING VIEWERS SOCIETY OF AMERICA

You Have the Effrontery to Call Yourself a
FILMMAKER!!!

Dear_____,

You Have the Nerve to Call Yourself an
EDITOR!!!

Dear Hack,

The Society of Discriminating Readers Ltd.

You Have the Nerve to Call Yourself a
WRITER!!!

Dear Hack,

The "Can't add two & two" Society of America

You have the gall to call yourself an
ACCOUNTANT!!!

Dear_____,

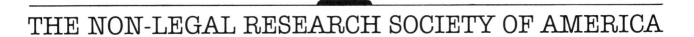

You Have the Effrontery to Call Yourself a
LAWYER!!!

Dear Shyster,

You have the nerve to call yourself a
DOCTOR!!!

Dear Quack,

The "Strike Terror in Their Hearts" Organization

This letter will self·destruct in five seconds... unless you read it!

Dear _____,

THE
"STRIKE FEAR IN THEIR HEARTS" SOCIETY

DON'T YOU DARE
THROW THIS AWAY!

Dear _____,

THE ORGANIZATION OF MALE CHAUVINIST PIGS LTD.

DEAR _____,

SAME TO YOU, BITCH!

THE
"I DIDN'T ORDER THIS"
SOCIETY OF AMERICA

I'M RETURNING YOUR

_____ !

Dear _____ ,

SOPHISTICATED RESTAURANT
CUSTOMERS
INC.

The food in your establishment
makes a "hot dog" seem
like a gourmet meal!

The No-Letterhead Association of America

I DON'T HAVE A LETTERHEAD, SO I'M FAKING YOU OUT WITH THIS FANCY TYPEFACE.

Dear Easily Fooled:

The Class Act
Society of America

Up Yours

Dear _____,

I'M SPEECHLESS...

...that's why I'm writing.

The Brilliant Retort Society of America

Dear Ignorant:

  Here is my brilliant retort: _____

_____

_____

The Quick-Witted Response Association of America

SAME TO YOU... FELLA!

The
"I'VE HAD ENOUGH"
Organization of America

I'VE HAD ENOUGH OF YOUR

I WAITED ALL DAY!

DEAR ☐ JERK
      ☐ FORGETFUL CLOD
      ☐ UNTRUTHFUL PERSON
      ☐ UNFEELING HUMAN
      ☐ _____

YOU PROMISED TO BE AT MY HOME ON:

☐ MON. ☐ TUES. ☐ WED. ☐ THURS. ☐ FRI. ☐ SAT. ☐ SUN.

IN THE ☐ A.M. ☐ P.M.

YOU NEVER SHOWED UP!

NO MORE *Patience* **&** *Fortitude*, INC.

DISGRUNTLED MOVIEGOERS ASSOCIATION

Dear Theater Owner,

   I attended your theater recently and was subjected to:

   ☐ Sticky seats
   ☐ Dirty floors
   ☐ Knee-deep popcorn
   ☐ Sound too low   ☐ Sound too loud
   ☐ No picture (projectionist asleep)
   ☐ No focus (projectionist blind)
   ☐ Loud patron
   ☐ Theater too hot (no air conditioning)
   ☐ Theater too cold (too much air conditioning)
   ☐ _____

Therefore_____

_____

_____

                              _____

DISCRIMINATING LISTENERS SOCIETY

OF AMERICA

Dear _____,

Your Speech Was

☐ FASCINATING ☐ BORING ☐ BRILLIANT ☐ DULL

☐ TOO SHORT ☐ TOO LONG ☐ STUPID ☐ ASININE ☐ IRRELEVANT

☐ _____

STILL WAITING!

DEAR

☐ PLUMBER   ☐ ELECTRICIAN   ☐ FURNITURE DELIVERY MAN

☐ TELEPHONE MAN   ☐ CABLE TV MAN   ☐ _____

IT HAS BEEN   ☐ 1 WEEK   ☐ 2 WEEKS   ☐ 3 WEEKS   ☐ 3 MONTHS

☐ 3 YEARS   ☐ FOREVER   ☐ _____

Therefore:

NEW YORK
MAR. 11 '83
N Y
E R METER
683409

U.S. POSTAGE
83

The Unsolicited Mail Society of America

STOP SENDING

☞ ☐ YOUR BOOKS ☐ YOUR RECORDS ☐ JUNK MAIL

Dear_____,

COMPUTER ANTAGONISTS
ASSOCIATION OF AMERICA

DO NOT FOLD, SPINDLE OR MUTILATE!!!

DEAR _____

DISGRUNTLED EMPLOYEES
ASSOCIATION

DEAR BOSS:

TAKE THIS JOB AND SHOVE IT!

BECAUSE:

☐ YOU'RE CHEAP   ☐ YOU'RE OVERBEARING   ☐ YOU MAKE PASSES

☐ YOU'RE BORING   ☐ I'M SMARTER THAN YOU

☐ YOU YELL   ☐ I JUST DON'T LIKE YOU

☐ I DIDN'T GET A RAISE   ☐ _____

YOUR EX-EMPLOYEE _____

The "Had Enough" Association of America

Dear_____ ,

NO MORE EXCUSES!

The
Suitable For
Any Occasion
Society of America

Dear _____,

The *I Bought Your*

Book

Association

Mr. Gene Light
Rockefeller Center Station P.O.
P.O. Box 604
New York, N.Y. 10185

Dear Gene,

I ☐ Bought ☐ Borrowed ☐ Stole   your book.

It was ☐ terrific ☐ awful ☐ useful ☐ a waste of money

☐ needed more ideas   ☐ _____

My suggestion for more letterheads is: _____

_____

_____

_____

I understand that if my suggestion is used in
a future edition of "LETTERHEADS TO MAKE
YOUR POINT" I will receive a free copy of the
book as payment in full.

_____
SIGNED

_____
ADDRESS

_____
CITY/STATE/ZIP